IT'S COOL TO LEARN ABOUT COUNTRIES

Social Studies Explorer

GERMANY

◆ by Vicky Franchino

CHERRY LAKE PUBLISHING • ANN ARBOR, MICHIGAN

Published in the United States of America
by Cherry Lake Publishing
Ann Arbor, Michigan
www.cherrylakepublishing.com

Content Adviser: Harold James, PhD, Professor of History and
International Affairs, Princeton University, Princeton, New Jersey

Book design: The Design Lab

Photo credits: Cover, ©iStockphoto.com/raclro; page 4, ©Maugli/Shutterstock, Inc.; page
5, ©Ralph Loesche/Shutterstock, Inc.; page 9, ©Chris P./Shutterstock, Inc.; page 11,
page 19, and page 28, ©imagebroker/Alamy; page 12, ©Bernhard Classen/Alamy ; page
14, ©Felinda/Dreamstime.com; page 15, ©Classic Image/Alamy; page 16 and page 18
©The Print Collector/Alamy; page 17, ©akg-images/Alamy; page 22, ©Justin Leighton/
Alamy; page 23, ©tovovan/Shutterstock, Inc.; page 24, ©Alexandru Dobre/Dreamstime.
com ; page 25, ©iStockphoto.com/Dr. Heinz Linke; page 29, ©RicoK/Shutterstock, Inc.;
page 30, ©gary718/Shutterstock, Inc.; page 31, ©iStockphoto.com/Ralf Siegele; page
33, ©Kzenon/Shutterstock, Inc.; page 34, ©LianeM/Shutterstock, Inc.; page 35, ©Farzin
Salimi/Dreamstime.com; page 38, ©Vladimir Lukovic/Dreamstime.com; page 39, ©Cogipix/
Shutterstock, Inc.; page 41, ©iStockphoto.com/Ina Peters; page 42, ©Charlotte Lake/
Dreamstime.com.

Library of Congress Cataloging-in-Publication Data
Franchino, Vicky.
  It's cool to learn about countries. Germany/by Vicky Franchino.
      p. cm.—(Social studies explorer)
  Includes index.
  ISBN-13: 978-1-61080-098-3 (library binding)
  ISBN-10: 1-61080-098-2 (library binding) 1. Germany—Juvenile literature. I. Title.
II. Title: Germany.
  DD17.F724 2012
  943—dc22   2010053944

Cherry Lake Publishing would like to acknowledge the work of The Partnership for
21st Century Skills. Please visit www.21stcenturyskills.org for more information.

Printed in the United States of America
Corporate Graphics Inc.
July 2011
CLFA09

TABLE OF CONTENTS

CHAPTER ONE

WELCOME TO GERMANY!

❖ Some of Germany's castles are hundreds of years old.

Would you like to go to a country where the castles are real and not just in amusement parks? Where there are dark and mysterious woods that feel like those in fairy tales? Where people celebrate the month of October in September? Then you might like to visit Germany.

In some ways, Germany might seem similar to where you live. It has four seasons, which fall at the same time as seasons do in North America. For example, summer in Germany is during June, July, and August. Germany also has many of the same animals and plants that are found in North America. Deer, squirrels, and rabbits live in the woods amid the fir, oak, and beech trees.

Germany's forests are home to many of the same plants and animals found in North American forests.

Arctic Ocean
ASIA
GERMANY
EUROPE
Atlantic Ocean
Mediterranean Sea
Indian Ocean
AFRICA
Atlantic Ocean

This map shows where Germany is located on the continent of Europe.

Germany covers 137,847 square miles (357,022 square kilometers). That is slightly smaller than the state of Montana. Travel across Germany and you'll find many different types of landscapes. The southern part of the country is home to the Alps, a great mountain range that stretches across south-central Europe. Germany's highest point, the Zugspitze, rises 9,718 feet (2,962 meters) in the Alps.

In southwestern Germany, you'll find the Black Forest. This mountainous region is covered in thick forest that stretches more than 2,300 square miles (6,000 sq km). It gets its name from the dense, dark trees that grow there, which make the forest seem a bit scary!

The brothers Grimm, Jacob and Wilhelm, are two of the world's best-known storytellers. In the 1800s, the brothers wrote down the **traditional** fairy tales of Germany. You probably know some of them, including "Little Red Riding Hood," "Snow White," and "Rumpelstiltskin." The versions told by the brothers Grimm were scarier than today's versions. Although these stories might not have been set in the Black Forest, it would have been a good, spooky choice!

Little Red Riding Hood and Big Bad Wolf

More mountains rise in the middle of the country. This region is also home to valleys where farmers grow wheat, barley, corn, cherries, and grapes for wine.

Germany is famous for its highway, or autobahn, system. The autobahn is famed for having no speed limit, but the truth is, parts of it do. Most stretches of highway have a recommended speed limit of 80 miles (130 kilometers) per hour. In some places, the speed limit is slower. Some places also have speed limits that are only enforced during rain or snow. These limits might be as low as 37 mph (60 kph). Still, people from around the world travel to Germany just to take a drive down the autobahn!

Some of Europe's most important rivers run through Germany. The Rhine River is 820 miles (1,320 km) long, stretching from the Alps in Switzerland to the North Sea. It is the longest river in Germany. Many boats travel up and down the Danube River, bringing goods to the cities of Europe and beyond. The Danube starts in the Black Forest and flows east through 10 countries before ending at the Black Sea, on the border between Europe and Asia.

The city of Passau is one of the many located along the Danube River.

Germany is made up of 16 Länder, which are like the states in the United States. The country's capital, Berlin, lies in the northeast. Other major cities in Germany include Hamburg, Munich (München), Cologne (Köln), and Frankfurt. As you can see, we call some German cities by one name, and Germans call them by another! Trace the map on a separate piece of paper. Use an atlas or find a map online to label each of the 16 Länder, and use a star to represent Berlin.

CHAPTER TWO

BUSINESS AND GOVERNMENT

Police officers and other service workers help to make life better for the people of Germany.

What types of jobs do people have in Germany? About two-thirds of the people work in a service industry. This means that instead of growing crops or making products, they perform services for other people. Teachers, lawyers, police officers, and bus drivers are all service workers.

❖ German workers build everything from cars to solar panels.

Manufacturing is also important in Germany. The country produces chemicals, machinery, metals such as iron, and some of the world's greatest cars. Famous car manufacturers in Germany include Volkswagen, Mercedes, and BMW. Some Germans work in farming or the lumber industry, but these industries are small compared to services and manufacturing.

IMPORT EXPORT

Do you want to know more about Germany's economy? Take a look at its trading partners. Trading partners are countries that buy and sell products from one another. Goods that a country buys from another country are called imports. Goods sold to another country are called exports. Here is a graph showing the countries that are Germany's top trading partners.

IMPORTS ⟶ GERMANY ⟶ EXPORTS

IMPORTS
NETHERLANDS
CHINA
FRANCE
UNITED STATES
ITALY
UNITED KINGDOM
BELGIUM

0   2%   4%   6%   8%   10%

EXPORTS
FRANCE
UNITED STATES
NETHERLANDS
UNITED KINGDOM
ITALY
AUSTRIA
CHINA

0   2%   4%   6%   8%   10%   12%

Today, Germany is a **stable** country. Most people can find jobs and have a middle-class lifestyle. This means they are neither rich nor poor. But Germany has not always been a stable place.

What is now Germany was once home to many different tribes. As these tribes settled down, towns and kingdoms grew. During the period known as the First Reich, or First Empire (800 to 1806), there were many towns and kingdoms in the area that is now Germany.

Many of Germany's buildings have been around since the early days of the country's history.

After he united Germany, Otto von Bismarck served as its leader for 19 years.

By the 1800s, one of the most powerful states in the region was called Prussia. During the 18th century, Prussia's King Frederick II fought to make his country an important power in Europe. Dreams of creating a **unified** German empire followed. Otto von Bismarck, who became Prussia's prime minister in 1862, was determined to make this dream a reality. He united Germany in 1871.

During World War I, Germany was led by Kaiser Wilhelm II.

Germany's Second Reich (1871–1918) was during an uncertain time in Europe. Countries were friends one day and enemies the next, and eventually war broke out. Nearly all of Europe was involved in World War I (1914–1918), with Germany leading a group of countries fighting against a group led by Great Britain, France, and Russia. The United States joined the fight against Germany in 1917. Germany lost the war. A peace **treaty** forced Germany to pay a huge amount of money to cover the damages it caused during the war. Germany also had to give up land and get rid of almost all its military.

After World War I, Germany was in terrible shape. Its money became almost worthless. People didn't have jobs. The country and the government were in **chaos**. One man saw an opportunity in this situation. His name was Adolf Hitler.

Hitler led a political group called the Nazi Party. He convinced Germans that he could save the country. Hitler claimed that Jewish people were responsible for Germany's problems, and he said that he could make the country great again.

•➛ Hitler used the German people's anger over the results of World War I to gain control of the country.

Although not all Germans agreed with Hitler, he had enough support to gain control of the government. He created what is called the Third Reich (1933–1945). Within months of coming to power, Hitler began **persecuting** Jewish people. At first, Jewish people were forced from their jobs and businesses. In the following years, millions were killed or sent to **concentration camps**. Many tried to escape but found nowhere to go. Hitler also tried to expand Germany's boundaries. His efforts to take over large parts of Europe led to World War II (1939–1945) and the deaths of tens of millions of people.

Through murder and starvation, Hitler killed roughly 6 million Jewish people and another 5 million to 6 million other "undesirables." These included Russian prisoners of war, Gypsies, Jehovah's Witnesses, the mentally ill, and the handicapped. This mass murder is known as the Holocaust.

● Over time, protestors covered the Berlin Wall with graffiti.

In 1945 a group of countries called the Allies defeated Germany. The four major Allies—Great Britain, France, the **Soviet Union**, and the United States—had to decide what would happen to Germany. They decided to help the Germans rebuild. Germany was divided into four sections. Each of the major Allies was in charge of one section.

The United States, Great Britain, and France were capitalist countries, where people controlled their own businesses. The Soviet Union was a communist country, where the government controlled businesses and the economy. After World War II, the Soviet Union took over large portions of Eastern Europe, and the other Allies feared it would take over Germany.

The capitalist Allies put their zones together and created one country, the Federal Republic of Germany, or West Germany. The Soviet's region was called the German Democratic Republic, or East Germany.

Many people in East Germany wanted to leave. The region's economy was not doing well, and people had less political freedom than in West Germany. Because so many people tried to escape, the Soviets placed fences and explosives along the border. The capital city of Berlin was also divided in two. In 1961 the Soviets built a wall that separated East Berlin from West Berlin.

ACTIVITY

Go online and find a map of how Germany was divided after World War II. Look for Berlin, the capital city. Think of how hard it would be to live in a divided country and a divided city. During the Berlin Blockade (June 1948–May 1949), the Soviet Union tried to block all food and supplies from getting to West Berlin so they could control the city. The Allies used planes to help the people of West Berlin. This is known as the Berlin Airlift.

In the 1980s, the Soviet Union began to allow more freedom of speech and democracy. This led to the fall of the Berlin Wall in 1989. East and West Germany were reunited as one country on October 3, 1990. This date is now German Unity Day.

People from East Germany flooded into West Germany, where they were willing to work for lower wages than the people who already lived there. In East Germany, many buildings and roads were old. It was expensive to fix them. Some places were dangerously polluted. Reuniting the two parts of Germany was not easy.

❖ The fall of the Berlin Wall was celebrated by Germans throughout the country.

Germany is one of 27 countries that make up the European Union, or EU. The EU countries are tied together economically and politically. Many EU countries now use the same money, the euro. This means that when people travel from one European country to another, they often do not have to convert their money into a different **currency**.

Today, Germany has a democratic government called a federal republic. This means the country has a central government that is elected by its citizens. Germans who are 18 or older can vote, but they don't vote directly for their country's leader. Instead, they vote for people who will serve in the Bundestag, which is similar to the U.S. House of Representatives. The Bundestag chooses the chancellor, whose job is basically the same as the American president's. There is also a president, but the job doesn't hold a lot of power. Members of the Bundestag and **delegates** from the 16 Länder elect the president. The chancellor is elected for a 4-year term and the president for a 5-year term.

The legislature, the part of the government that makes the laws, includes the Bundestag and the Bundesrat, which represents all the Länder. There is also a judicial branch that helps interpret Germany's laws.

Angela Merkel is the first female chancellor of Germany. Although Merkel was born in West Germany, her father, a Lutheran minister, was sent to East Germany. Religious people were not always treated well in East Germany. When Germany was reunified, Merkel joined the government. She was elected chancellor in 2005 and reelected in 2009.

MEET THE PEOPLE

◦ German students study many subjects in school.

Most people in Germany have similar backgrounds. About 90 percent are **descended** from the tribes that once lived throughout northern Europe. The rest come from other European countries, including Turkey. Many Turkish people and people of other nationalities came to Germany in the 1950s and 1960s as "guest workers."

German is the national language of the country, but there are different German **dialects**. High German began in the northwestern part of Germany, and today it is considered the proper way to write and speak German. Low German was originally spoken more in southern Germany and is not as common today. In German all nouns are capitalized, unlike in English. Also, German words are often put together to make very long compound words. One of the longest has 63 letters: *Rindfleischetikettierungsüberwachungsaufgabenübertragungsgesetz*. It is a law related to the labeling of beef, so it doesn't get used too often!

Did you know that most German children know multiple languages and that they all learn English in school? If you met a German person your age, you could probably have a conversation in English!

GERMAN

There are a number of German words that are very similar to English. See if you can match the words!

GERMAN	ENGLISH
1. Haus	a. Friend
2. Schokolade	b. Glass
3. Mann	c. Shoe
4. Glas	d. House
5. Freund	e. Night
6. Schuh	f. Chocolate
7. Nacht	g. Man

STOP Don't write in this book!

Answers: 1-d; 2-f; 3-g; 4-b; 5-a; 6-c; 7-e

Education is important in Germany, and almost everyone in the country can read. Children start school when they are about 6 years old and go to *Grundschule*, or elementary school, for 4 years. When they are about 10 years old, students take a special exam to learn what kind of school they will go to next.

Some students go to *Hauptschule* (grades 5–9). This prepares them to attend vocational school where they'll learn to do a specific job, such as plumbing. Other students go to *Realschule* (grades 5–10). Students with the highest test scores are sent to *Gymnasium* (grades 5–13). This prepares students for college.

German students usually go to school about 200 days a year. They have a 6-week break in the summer, with shorter breaks spread throughout the year. The school day usually ends around noon or 1:00 p.m., giving students the rest of the day free!

Books are so common today that it's easy to forget they used to be rare and expensive. Johannes Gutenberg was one of the people who helped make books affordable. Gutenberg was born in the late 1300s. He spent much of his life creating a printing press. It took Gutenberg many years—and he had many struggles along the way—but in the 1450s, he published a Bible. About 40 copies of the Gutenberg Bible still exist today.

❖ A statue of Martin Luther was erected in the German city of Dresden.

MARTIN LUTHER

Religion was traditionally very important in Germany. The first German tribes followed **pagan** religions. Christianity began to be popular around the fourth century, when the Romans entered the region.

Catholicism was the most common religion in Germany until the 1500s. At that time, a priest named Martin Luther (1483–1546) began to question some of the Catholic Church's practices. Church leaders were unhappy with Luther and forced him to leave the Catholic Church. Luther and others started a new branch of Christianity, called Protestantism. It gets its name from the word *protest*.

Today, about 34 percent of Germans are Protestants and 34 percent are Catholics. More than 20 percent of the people do not belong to a religion, and about 4 percent are Muslims. There are about 100,000 Jewish people in Germany today, but there were about 5 times that many before World War II.

↔ The Holocaust Memorial in Berlin pays tribute to the millions of Jewish people killed during World War II.

CELEBRATIONS

↝ Karneval parades often feature people wearing a variety of interesting costumes.

In Germany many holidays are tied to religious events. Germans use these holidays as a time to get together with family and friends.

HOLIDAYS

January 1	New Year's Day
January 6	Epiphany
March or April	Good Friday
March or April	Easter
March or April	Easter Monday
April or May	Ascension Day
May 1	Labor Day
May	Whit Monday
October 3	German Unity Day
December 25	Christmas Day
December 26	St. Stephen's Day

Karneval, or Fasching, is a celebration that comes right before Lent, a somber 40-day period during which Christians remember the last days of Jesus's life. People celebrate Karneval with costumes, parades, and dances. Lent ends with Easter. For Easter, families decorate their homes with fresh flowers and small trees trimmed with eggs. Children dye eggs and search to find their treats from the Easter bunny!

Oktoberfest is another big celebration. You might guess that it happens in October, but it usually starts in September! The first Oktoberfest was held in the city of Munich in October 1810 when Prince Ludwig of Bavaria got married. The prince decided to invite everyone to his wedding, and Oktoberfest was born. During Oktoberfest some men wear *Lederhosen*, which are leather shorts with suspenders. A woman might wear a *Dirndl*, a dress with a blouse under it and an apron over it. People dance the *Schuhplattler*, which includes slapping the soles of their shoes! Oktoberfest isn't a 1-day celebration—it can last more than 2 weeks!

◆ Wearing traditional clothing is a fun part of celebrating Oktoberfest.

The Christmas holidays are very special in Germany. On the night of December 5, Sankt Nikolaus, or Saint Nicholas, fills children's shoes with treats and small gifts. Sometimes, Sankt Nikolaus delivers presents personally, in exchange for a dance or song. Most families decorate a Christmas tree. In Germany it is called a *Tannenbaum*.

The year ends with a New Year's Eve celebration called *Silvester*. Germans celebrate with fireworks, dancing, and tasty food, such as filled doughnuts called *Berliners*!

◆ Some Germans go all out when it comes time to decorate for Christmas.

➻ Germans are very supportive of their national football team.

In their free time, Germans often visit museums or attend concerts. Some of the world's most famous **composers** were from Germany, including Johann Sebastian Bach (1685–1750), George Frideric Handel (1685–1759), and Ludwig van Beethoven (1770–1827).

Germans like to hike and are passionate about sports, especially soccer, which they call *Fussball* (football). Germany's national football team is usually very good. The German team has often competed in the World Cup, a competition of the world's best teams.

MAKE A SCHULTÜTE!

A German child going into the first grade receives a Schultüte. This is a decorated paper cone that is filled with small presents, candy, and school supplies. Make this for someone you know who's starting school!

MATERIALS

- 1 sheet of poster board
- Pencil
- Glue or glue stick
- Tissue paper
- String
- Scissors
- Packing tape
- Ribbon
- Stickers, feathers, beads, crayons, markers, glitter

STEP ONE →

INSTRUCTIONS

1. Lay the poster board on a table. Take the string and tie it snugly around the pencil, near the bottom. Hold the loose end of the string at the bottom left corner of the poster board. Pull the pencil with the string attached out in a straight line toward the bottom right corner. Keeping the string stretched tightly, draw a quarter circle from the bottom right corner to the left side of the poster board.

2. Cut out the shape and decorate one side of the poster board. Let your imagination go wild! You can use stickers, feathers, or beads; draw with crayons or markers; or sprinkle glitter.

3. Turn the poster board over so that the decorated side is down. Position it so that the point is at the bottom.

4. Put glue on the left straight side of the paper. Carefully roll the paper into a cone. Use the tape to hold the cone in place. Try taping the inside of the cone, to make it look nicer.

5. Unfold the tissue paper, and staple or tape it to the top of the cone. Make sure the tissue paper extends a few inches above the top of the cone. Fill the cone with goodies (nothing too heavy or it will break!). Cut off a piece of ribbon and tie it around the tissue paper to close the top of your Schultüte. Give your Schultüte to your favorite student or friend!

CHAPTER FIVE

WHAT'S FOR DINNER?

➝ Honey is a healthy way to add some sweetness to a meal.

If you're traveling to Germany, bring your appetite with you. There are many delicious things to eat—and many times to eat them!

The day starts with *Frühstück*, or breakfast. Most people eat fresh rolls with honey or jam. Yogurt is

popular and so is *Quark*, a cross between yogurt and cottage cheese. Hungry in the middle of the morning? It's time for *Zweites Frühstück*, which translates to "second breakfast." Most schoolchildren eat bread, yogurt, or granola bars. *Mittagessen*, or lunch, traditionally includes hot food and is the biggest meal of the day.

↝ Quark is used in a variety of German dishes. Here is is mixed with herbs.

In the afternoon, especially on the weekends, people like to get together for *Kaffee und Kuchen*, coffee and cake. They might go to a *Konditorei* for a delicious fancy dessert. The last meal of the day is *Abendessen*. This is a cold meal that's similar to Frühstück and usually includes fresh rolls, cold meats, and cheese.

Bread is important in Germany, and almost every neighborhood has its own bakery. Pumpernickel bread is popular. It is heavy and dark—almost the color of coffee—and made from a type of grain called rye.

Do you enjoy pretzels? Then you have something in common with many Germans. No one can say for sure when and where pretzels were first made, but they are a favorite bread for many people in Germany.

pretzels

❖ Sausage and sauerkraut is a popular dish in Germany.

German families enjoy having their evening meal together, and the table is usually set with a tablecloth, cloth napkins, and nice dishes. Germans use a knife and fork for almost all foods—even sandwiches and pizza.

In Germany, there is always something good to eat and always something to celebrate. There is much to do and see in Germany. Happy travels!

◦▸ Strudel is a popular German treat made with thin layers of pastry and fruit fillings.

ACTIVITY RECIPE

GERMANY

Apfelpfannekuchen is an apple pancake that is perfect for a birthday or holiday breakfast. The recipe requires a hot stove and a hot, heavy pan. Have an adult help you with these.

Apfelpfannekuchen

INGREDIENTS

6 tablespoons butter

2 large tart apples, peeled and sliced

3 tablespoons (45 ml) lemon juice

1/2 teaspoon (2 ml) cinnamon

5 tablespoons (75 ml) powdered sugar, plus extra for sprinkling

3 eggs

1/4 teaspoon (1 ml) salt

1/2 cup (125 grams) flour

1/2 cup (125 ml) milk

INSTRUCTIONS

1. Preheat the oven to 425 degrees Fahrenheit (218 degrees Celsius).

2. Melt the butter in a heavy cast-iron frying pan that can go in the oven.

3. Take out 2 tablespoons of the butter and put it in a medium-size bowl.

4. Put the apple slices in another bowl. Mix them with the lemon juice, then add the cinnamon and sugar. Stir until the apples are coated.

5. Put the apples into the frying pan. Cook over medium heat until the apples are cooked but not mushy. This will probably take about 5 minutes. Remove the pan from the heat, but leave the apples in the pan.

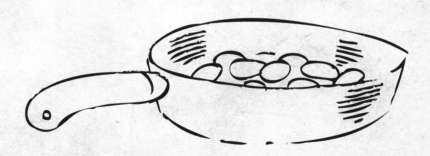

6. Add the eggs, salt, flour, and milk to the bowl with the melted butter. Beat with a whisk until it becomes a smooth batter.

7. Make sure the cooked apples are spread evenly over the bottom of the frying pan. Pour the batter over the apples.

8. Have an adult put the pan into the oven for you. Bake for about 20 minutes.

9. When your pancake is golden and puffy, it's time to eat. Have an adult flip it onto a plate. Then sprinkle it with powdered sugar.

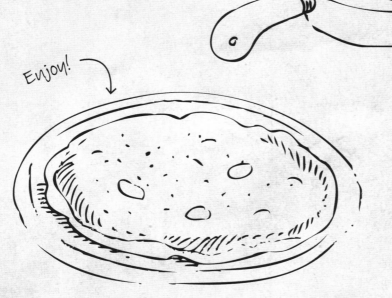

Enjoy!

GLOSSARY

chaos (KAY-oss) confusion and disorder

composers (kum-PO-zurz) people who write music

concentration camps (kon-sun-TRAY-shun KAMPS) prisons where persecuted people are kept, usually during a war

currency (KUR-unt-see) paper money or coins

delegates (DEL-uh-gitz) people who speak or act for others

descended (dee-SEND-ed) came from a certain source

dialects (DYE-uh-lekts) forms of language used only in a certain place

manufacturing (man-yuh-FAK-chur-ing) the making of products, often with the use of equipment

pagan (PAY-gun) related to religions with many gods

persecuting (PUR-si-kyoot-ing) harassing or trying to injure

Soviet Union (SOW-vee-et YOON-yun) a country made up of Russia and other parts of eastern Europe and northern Asia that existed from 1922 to 1991

stable (STAY-bul) not likely to change

traditional (truh-DI-shun-ul) relating to a belief or custom that is handed down

treaty (TREE-tee) an agreement between countries

unified (YOON-ih-fyde) made into one, united

FOR MORE INFORMATION

Books

Byers, Ann. *Germany: A Primary Source Cultural Guide.*
New York: PowerPlus Books, 2005.

Goulding, Sylvia. *Germany.* New York: Chelsea Clubhouse,
2008.

Smith, Jeremy. *The Fall of the Berlin Wall.* Milwaukee:
World Almanac Library, 2004.

Web Sites

Central Intelligence Agency—The World Factbook: Germany
*www.cia.gov/library/publications/the-world-factbook/geos/
gm.html*
This is a great resource for information about Germany's
geography, economy, and more.

National Geographic Kids—Germany
kids.nationalgeographic.com/kids/places/find/germany/
This site is full of videos, maps, pictures, and more.

TIME for Kids—Germany
*www.timeforkids.com/TFK/kids/hh/goplaces/
article/0,28376,1147393,00.html*
This site has photos and maps, plus a section where you
can hear how German words are pronounced!

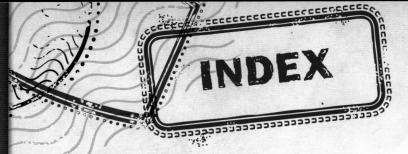

INDEX

ABOUT THE AUTHOR

Vicky Franchino's ancestors came from Germany, which is why she thought it would be interesting to learn more about the country. She learned German when she was in high school and has been to Germany twice. Vicky would like you to know that German food is as delicious as it looks! She lives in Madison, Wisconsin, with her family and hopes to go to Germany again someday.